Citizenship

Being Honest

Cassie Mayer

Curious Fox

Curious Fox is an imprint of Capstone Global Library Limited,
7 Pilgrim Street, London, EC4V 6LB – Registered company
number: 6695582

www.curious-fox.com

Editorial: Cassie Mayer and Charlotte Guillain
Design: Joanna Hinton-Malivoire
Illustrated by Mark Beech
Art editor: Ruth Blair

ISBN 978 1 782 02296 1
18 17 16
10 9 8 7 6 5 4 3

A CIP catalogue for this book is available from the British
Library.

Printed and bound in China by Golden Cup Printing Co. , Ltd

Contents

Being honest means telling
the truth.

Being honest means people can trust you.

When you return something that is not yours ...

you are being honest.

When you own up to making a mess …

you are being honest.

When you tell someone you made a mistake ...

you are being honest.

When you say,
"I've had my share" …

you are being honest.

When you say,
"I've had my turn" ...

you are being honest.

When you tell someone how
you feel ...

you are being honest.

When you admit that you
were wrong ...

you are being honest.

Being honest is important.

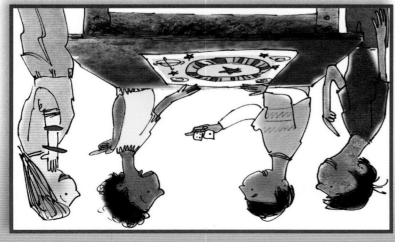

How can you be honest?

How is this boy being honest?

Activity

Picture glossary

admit tell something that you may be afraid to tell

honest always telling the truth

trust to believe in someone

Index